the parenting children course

for those parenting 0 to 10-year-olds

> Guest Manual

Contents

This manual is designed to be used on The Parenting Children Course with the DVDs or live talks. See page 80 for more information on how to join or run a course.

Acknowledgements

We are very grateful indeed to the following people for their help and encouragement in the creation of The Parenting Children Course:

Rob Parsons, for his inspiration, stories and illustrations in his books and talks.

Ross Campbell, for the insights in his books, especially on managing anger.

Gary Chapman, for the help that his concept of the five love languages has been to us and many other parents.

Nicky and Sila Lee

The authors and publisher gratefully acknowledge permission to reproduce copyright material in this book. Every effort has been made to trace and contact copyright holders. If there are any inadvertent omissions we apologise to those concerned and will ensure that a suitable acknowledgement is made in all future editions.

The table 'Recommended hours of sleep' (p. 13) is from Sue Palmer, *Toxic Childhood*, Orion Books, 2006 and reproduced by permission of the publisher.

The diagram (p. 32) is from Sue Palmer, *Toxic Childhood*, Orion Books, 2006 and reproduced by permission of the publisher.

The SMART rules for staying safe online (p. 59) are copyright © Childnet International 2002-2011 and are reproduced with permission. **childnet.com**

1 Building Strong Foundations

Part 1 The role of the family

Introduction

- any expectations to be perfect parents are unrealistic and unhelpful
- no instant recipe or formula for bringing up children
- different situations and different children call for different approaches
- some general principles that apply to all families
- value of discussions with other parents
- challenge of pace of life today
- vital for parents to invest enough time and energy into family life

The Parenting Children Wheel

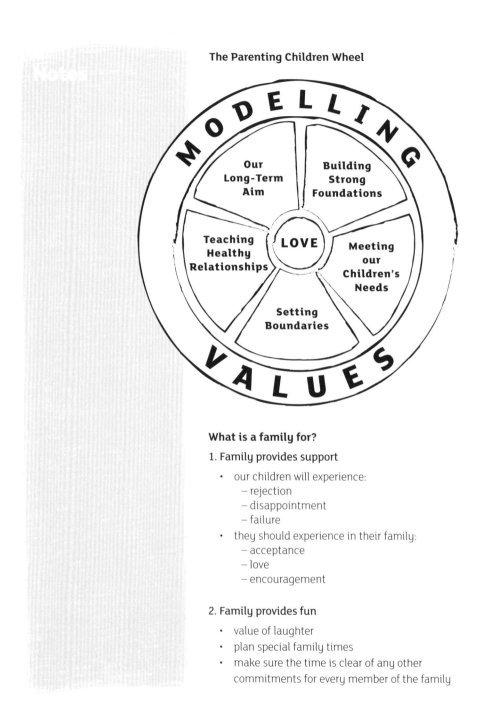

What is a family for?

1. Family provides support

- our children will experience:
  - – rejection
  - – disappointment
  - – failure
- they should experience in their family:
  - – acceptance
  - – love
  - – encouragement

2. Family provides fun

- value of laughter
- plan special family times
- make sure the time is clear of any other commitments for every member of the family

- prevent interruptions from the telephone or other people (unless they are invited with the understanding that it is 'family time')

Suggested routine for family times
- try to make it the same time each week
  - spend at least an hour and a half having fun
  - take it in turns to choose what activity you do
    (see 'Suggested activities' in the Homework Exercise 1 pages 19–20)

- have it around a meal
- get each family member in turn to choose their favourite menu – when they are old enough, use it as an opportunity to teach them to cook their choice of food
- make sure conversation and activities are at the level of the children
- if it is a week night, work out when to fit in homework, music practice, etc (before or after depending on the age of the children)
- turn off the TV, or limit it to one programme or DVD that you can watch together

3. Family provides a moral compass
- children learn about good and bad behaviour from their family
- they learn values such as:
  - thinking about others
  - taking responsibility
  - helping around the house

4. Family is the place where children learn to relate
- children learn to relate through *experiencing*, *observing* and *practising* various relationships within the family:
  - parent–child
  - mother–father
  - sibling–sibling

– grandparents–grandchild
– uncles, aunts, cousins, etc

Experiencing: parent–child relationship

- children learn to love through experiencing their parents' unconditional love

> ' … There is no power on earth like unconditional love. And I think that if you offered that to your child, you're 90% of the way home. There may be days when you don't feel like it – it's not uncritical love; that's a different animal – but to know you can always come back, that is huge in life. That takes you a long, long way. And I would say that every parent out there that can extend that to their child at an early age, it's going to make for a better human being.'
>
> **Warren Buffett,** *Yahoo! News and The Huffington Post* 8 July 2010

- important for children to feel accepted for who they are
- our love and acceptance give our children confidence through building in them:
  - security (knowing they are loved not for what they do, but for who they are)
  - self-worth (knowing they are of value – their self-worth is based on what they think we, their parents, think of them)
  - significance (knowing there is a purpose to their lives, and that they have a worthwhile contribution to make)
- ultimately security, self-worth and significance come from God
  - we model God's parenthood of us
  - parents are in loco dei (in his place to represent him)

'We love because he first loved us.'

**1 John 4:19,
The Bible**

Observing: mother–father (and other adult) relationships

- children learn to relate through observing adult relationships
  - how we, their parents, speak and listen to each other
  - the physical affection we show
  - whether and how we resolve conflicts
- children need to see at close-hand the modelling of an intimate, committed adult relationship (for more information, go to relationshipcentral.org)
- if parenting together, consider doing The Marriage Course to invest in your relationship
- if not parenting together, work at having the best possible relationship with your child's other parent (resolving conflict, forgiveness, consistency, etc)

Practising: sibling–sibling (and other peer) relationships

- children learn to relate through practising with brothers, sisters and friends
  - how to play together
  - how to share
  - how to handle arguments
  - how to apologise and forgive

For 5- and 10-week courses
Exercise

Taking stock of your parenting

If you have a child who is old enough for the statements below to be relevant, fill the chart in for your own parenting. Otherwise, fill it in for the way you were parented yourself as a child (as we can find ourselves imitating what our parents did for us). Be honest! Then tell someone else what you would like to change.

	Tick the relevant box for each statement				
	Never	Rarely	Occasionally	Usually	Always
We have special time all together as a family at least once a week	☐	☐	☐	☐	☐
I spend some time each week doing something fun with my child(ren)	☐	☐	☐	☐	☐
We sit down around a table to eat together as a family (not in front of the TV) several times a week	☐	☐	☐	☐	☐
I regularly tell my child(ren) I love them and give them more praise than criticism	☐	☐	☐	☐	☐
I control the amount of time my child(ren) watch TV and play computer games	☐	☐	☐	☐	☐
I give my child(ren) the time and opportunity to talk to me; I listen to their concerns	☐	☐	☐	☐	☐
I know who my child(ren)'s friends are, what they enjoy doing at school, and their favourite food	☐	☐	☐	☐	☐
My child(ren) can talk openly with me and let me know if there are ways I have upset them	☐	☐	☐	☐	☐
I am in control of myself when disciplining my child(ren)	☐	☐	☐	☐	☐
I/we have worked out boundaries for my/our child(ren) and consistently enforce them	☐	☐	☐	☐	☐
I talk to my child(ren) about my beliefs and values	☐	☐	☐	☐	☐
I pray regularly for our child(ren) and am passing on spiritual values	☐	☐	☐	☐	☐
I discuss key parenting issues with my child(ren)'s mother/father and we work on a joint approach	☐	☐	☐	☐	☐

For 10-week course only
Small group discussion

1. Can you remember a special moment of receiving support from your family as you were growing up?

_____

_____

2. Did you have fun in your family when you were growing up? If so, when was this?

_____

_____

3. When do you have the most fun together as a family?

_____

_____

4. Where is your child learning most about how to build healthy relationships?

_____

_____

5. What could you do to invest in the various relationships in your family?

_____

_____

Homework – Complete **Exercise 1** on pages 19–20

Part 2 Patterns for a healthy family life

Setting goals

- having a vision for our family life
- pausing to think about what we want to achieve
- what will our children's memories be of us and their home in twenty years' time?

Goals for our family life

When they are adults, will our children associate their upbringing with:
- having fun together as a family?
- being listened to?
- being able to talk through difficult choices?
- being encouraged and affirmed?
- being valued for their unique personality and gifts?
- knowing they are loved?
- learning important values of honesty, generosity, etc?
- learning to think about others?
- being prayed for?
- having clear boundaries for their own protection?
- seeing kindness modelled?

---

1. The importance of play

'One major side effect of the technological revolution has been the replacement of age-old activities (running, climbing, pretending, making, sharing) with a solitary, sedentary screen-based lifestyle.'

Sue Palmer, *Toxic Childhood*

- using their imagination
- learning skills
- playing on their own
- playing with others

- indoor and outdoor play
- limiting screen time

TV recommended limits	
Child's age	Length of time
Under 3 years	no screen exposure
3 to 7 years old	30 to 60 minutes a day
7 to 12 years old	60 minutes a day
12 to 15 years old	90 minutes a day
16+ years old	2 hours a day

Source: Dr Aric Sigman

2. The importance of bonding

- for children, love is spelt 'T - I - M - E'
- children need quantity time as well as quality time
- significance of first eighteen months of a child's life
- who will be our child's main caregiver?
- can be hard to work out balance of parenting and employment
  - working at home/from home
  - full-time/part-time
- the time we spend with our children is more powerful in communicating our love than anything we say
- we need to **prioritise** our time
  - learning when to say 'yes' to our children and 'no' to other people and things
  - the only place we are indispensable is at home
- we need to **plan** our time
  - time with the people who are most precious to us doesn't just happen
  - if married, plan 'marriage time' each week
  - as a parent, plan 'family time' each week
  - plan some one-to-one time with each child (we will look at this in detail in Session 2 Part 2)

- we need to **protect** our time from
  - the TV
  - the telephone
  - other people
  - our work

3. Establishing routines

- routine brings security and safety
- children thrive on routine
- regular mealtimes
  - help to provide a healthy diet
  - give opportunities to be together as a family
  - many benefits of sitting around a table
- bedtime
  - important that children get enough sleep (see table below)
  - bath time, story time, prayer time
  - provides natural opportunities to talk to and pass on our values to our children
  - sets in place channels of communication on every level
    - emotional
    - physical
    - spiritual

Recommended hours of sleep		
	Age group	**Recommended hours of sleep (daily)**
Babies	3 to 11 months	14 to 15 hours
Toddlers	12 to 35 months	12 to 14 hours
Younger children	3 to 6 years old	11 to 13 hours
Older children	7 to 11 years old	10 to 11 hours

Source: Sue Palmer, *Toxic Childhood*

Small group discussion

1. Can you remember a special moment of receiving support from your family as you were growing up?

_____

_____

2. Did you have fun in your family as you were growing up? When do you have most fun together as a family now?

_____

_____

3. What demands on your time stop you from spending time with your children?

_____

_____

4. What routines have you developed in your family life? (*eg: a weekly 'family time' during the weekend, around mealtimes, at bedtime*)

_____

_____

5. What new routines would you like to develop?

_____

_____

Homework – complete **Exercises 1** and **2** on pages 19–22

For 10-week course only
Small group discussion

1. What is your main goal as a parent/carer of children?

_____

_____

2. What helps your child(ren) to engage in healthy play?

_____

_____

3. What demands on your time stop you from spending time with your children?

_____

_____

4. What routines have you developed in your family life? (*eg: a weekly 'family time', during the weekend, around mealtimes, at bedtime*)

_____

_____

5. What new routines would you like to develop?

_____

_____

Homework – complete **Exercise 2** on pages 21–22

Homework ✐

Exercise 1

Planning family time

Plan a family time this week (or as soon as possible):

On _____ (date) we will have a family time together.

Together as a family we plan to:

_____

_____

(Plan a special activity with your child(ren), or keep it as a surprise)

Suggested activities:
1. Go to the park; play football, cricket, frisbee, etc
2. Have a card, draughts or chess tournament
3. Play charades (children love seeing their parents being silly!)
4. Colour, draw or paint (try doing some portraits of each other)
5. Play with bricks, cars or soldiers
6. Play 'houses' or dressing up
7. Try cooking a new recipe together
8. Make or mend something together
9. Play 'hide-and-seek', 'hunt the thimble' or a similar game
10. Go for a family walk or bike ride
11. Go boating
12. Go on a picnic (when the weather's nice or even in the rain!)
13. Make pancakes together
14. Go rollerblading (wearing protective gear!)
15. Go swimming
16. Plan a scavenger hunt. Try to find something in the house for every letter of the alphabet
17. Read a good book aloud. (*eg: books like C. S. Lewis'* Chronicles of Narnia *series appeal to both children and adults*)
18. Look through photo albums or look at old family videos/DVDs
19. Make a recording of the most recent 'family news', and send it to a close friend or relative whom you don't see very often

Please turn over ⇨

Exercise 1 (continued)

20. Play a board game that all can enjoy – Monopoly, Scrabble, Sorry, Trivial Pursuit, etc
21. Sing favourite songs or nursery rhymes (perhaps with homemade musical instruments)
22. Make a collage using anything from old buttons and scrap material to pictures out of a magazine
23. Make a family website with photos and news
24. Make a simple bird feeder for the winter and hang it where everyone can see it
25. Make puppets and put on a puppet show
26. Have a barbecue and cook bananas in their skins – cut lengthways and stuffed with chocolate!
27. Visit an elderly person
28. Listen to a story CD (many fairytales, Bible stories, etc come with read-along books for little children)
29. Encourage younger children to draw and colour a picture to send to their grandparents. Older children could write a letter
30. Play tennis, basketball, golf or whatever sport your children enjoy
31. Take the children on a tour of the place where a parent works
32. Draw a family tree on paper and complete it as a family. Add photographs if you have them
33. Give each person a large piece of paper and take turns tracing the outlines of their bodies on it. Colour in the outlines to look like them
34. Gather a variety of leaves in the autumn and press them in a book
35. Plan to help a child in a developing country as a family
36. Go for a walk near your house to get to know your neighbourhood better
37. Put together a scrapbook describing a favourite holiday or any special event (with pictures, photos, writing, souvenirs, etc)
38. Write and act out a pantomime or play the 'adverb game' (which involves one member of the family doing an action on command and the rest of the family trying to try to guess the adverb, so you might have to mime eating your supper 'jerkily' or playing football 'clumsily'!)
39. Go out for an ice-cream, hot chocolate or a milkshake together

Other ideas:

_____

_____

_____

Exercise 2

Healthy habits

In what areas would you like to see change in your parenting?

1. My main goals as a parent are to

i. _____

ii. _____

iii. _____

2. Would your children benefit from more active/creative play?   Yes/No

If yes, I could encourage/allow my child(ren) to play more creatively by:

_____

3. What new routines (if any) would you like to introduce into your family life?
(*eg: a weekly 'family night', meals around a table, a bedtime routine, doing something special at the weekend or a family holiday*)

On a daily basis

• _____

• _____

On a weekly basis

• _____

• _____

Please turn over ⇨

Exercise 2 (continued)

On an annual basis

- _____

- _____

4. What demands on your time are likely to conflict with these routines?

- _____

- _____

- _____

5. What changes/sacrifices could you make so that these new routines become possible?

- _____

- _____

- _____

Meeting our Children's Needs

Review

Session 1 – Building Strong Foundations

What is a family for?
- a family provides support
- a family provides fun
- a family provides a moral compass
- a family provides a model for relating to others

Establishing a healthy family life
- healthy play
- healthy bonding
- healthy routines
  - daily: mealtimes/bedtimes
  - weekly: creating 'family time' to have fun together

> **Discuss:**
> What was most relevant for you from Session 1? Have you organised any 'family time' since then?

Part 1 – The five love languages: words and touch

Love in action
- self-confidence is built through knowing we are loved
- self-confidence enables us:

    – to be different when we need to be

    – to build close relationships

- our children have 'emotional tanks', which need to be kept full
- their behaviour acts as the gauge showing the level in the tank

Five ways of expressing love

(based on *The Five Love Languages of Children* by Gary Chapman and Ross Campbell)

1. Affirming words

- our words can affect how our children think about themselves for the rest of their lives
- don't give praise indiscriminately – look for attributes and actions to commend them for
- words of affirmation build them up and will affect their behaviour and achievement

> 'The golden rule is this: catch your kids red-handed doing something right and praise them for it.'
>
> **Steve Chalke,** *How to Succeed as a Parent*

- practise commending for success more than criticising for failure
- correct mistakes without condemning the child

2. Affectionate touch

- physical contact is vital to a child – for boys as much as girls
- a primary way of conveying our love for our child(ren)
- for some parents being demonstrative doesn't come naturally
- we can all learn
- create daily routines that involve physical affection

Exercise

Using words and touch

Fill in your answers to the two questions below and then discuss what you have put with one or two other people.

1. How natural do you find it to speak affirming words and to give affectionate touch to your child(ren)?

_____

_____

2. Does this relate to your own childhood experiences?

_____

_____

For 10-week course only
Small group discussion

1. What are the signs of an empty 'emotional tank' in your child(ren)?

_____

_____

2. Have you heard of the concept of the 'five love languages'?
   If so, how useful has it been to you in all your relationships?

_____

_____

Please turn over ⇨

3. How natural do you find it to speak affirming words to your child(ren)? Does this relate to your own experiences as a child?

_____

_____

4. What helps you as a parent to give more praise than criticism?

_____

_____

5. How natural is it for you to give affectionate touch to your child(ren)? Does this relate to your own childhood experiences?

_____

_____

Homework – complete **Exercises 1** and **2** on pages 31–32

Part 2 The five love languages: time, presents and actions

3. One-to-one time

- our children crave to be noticed by us and crave our attention
- special time with each child develops their self-esteem and their ability to relate to others
- can be difficult for us as parents to recognise this need and to fulfil it
- the more children we have, the more planning and conscious effort it takes
- channels of communication are opened through spending one-to-one time with our child(ren)
- can transform a child's behaviour
- eye contact:
  - can be used either positively or negatively
  - children learn by modelling – if we do it, they'll do it
  - easy when they are babies – but don't give up eye contact as they get older
  - good eye contact goes hand in hand with 'active listening'

> 'Eye contact is crucial not only in making good communicational contact with a child, but in filling his or her emotional needs.'
>
> Ross Campbell, *How to Really Love Your Child*

4. Thoughtful presents

- presents need not be expensive
- they can have a high emotional value
- not be used as a substitute for words, time or touch
- recognise when a child is expressing love through wanting to give you a present
- teach them the value of waiting for something ('delayed gratification')

5. Kind actions

- plenty of opportunities for parents!
- generally taken for granted by young children
- important to teach our children to show and express their gratitude for what we and others do for them
- worth checking our attitude — is it willing or resentful when we do things for our child(ren)?
- good to allow our children to express love through attempting kind, helpful actions

We need to express love to our child(ren) in all five ways

- some expressions of love/'love languages' will be more important to them than others
- as our children grow older we need to try to recognise their primary and secondary ways of feeling loved
- pay particular attention to using the principal love languages

Small group discussion

1. What are the signs of an empty 'emotional tank' in your child(ren)?

_____

_____

2. Do you have memories from your own childhood of receiving love from your parent(s) through any of the five love languages?

_____

_____

3. Which of the five (words, touch, time, presents, actions) was most important for you as a child to feel loved?

_____

_____

4. Which expressions of love do you think make the most difference to your child(ren)?

_____

_____

5. Which of the five do you find most difficult to give? What would help you show love in this way?

_____

_____

Homework – complete **Exercises 1–4** on pages 31–34

For 10-week course only
Small group discussion

1. Do you have memories from your own childhood of receiving love from your parent(s) through any of the five love languages?

_____

_____

2. Which of the five (words, touch, time, presents, actions) was most important for you as a child to feel loved?

_____

_____

3. Which expressions of love do you think make most difference to your child(ren)?

_____

_____

4. Which of the five do you find most difficult to give? What would help you show love in this way?

_____

_____

Homework – complete **Exercises 3** and **4** on pages 32–34

Homework 📝

Exercise 1

Ranking the five love languages

If your child(ren) is/are old enough, try to rank the five ways of expressing love in order of priority for them and for yourself/yourselves.

Yourself:

1. _____

2. _____

3. _____

4. _____

5. _____

Partner (if relevant):

1. _____

2. _____

3. _____

4. _____

5. _____

Child:

1. _____

2. _____

3. _____

4. _____

5. _____

Child (if relevant):

1. _____

2. _____

3. _____

4. _____

5. _____

(Do a similar list for any additional children)

- Check that you are showing love to your child(ren) through all five expressions of love
- Pay special attention to giving the two most important for each child

Exercise 2

Giving encouragement

Write a list of the affirming, encouraging remarks you have said to your child(ren) today (or yesterday), and then write a list of the critical remarks you have made.

Affirming remarks	Critical remarks

Which list is longer? If there are more critical words than affirming remarks, make a conscious effort to reverse the balance over this coming week.

Exercise 3

Childhood memories of one-to-one time

1. Write down any memories from your childhood when one or both of your parents (or the person/people who brought you up) spent time doing something special with you on your own

_____

_____

Exercise 3 (continued)

2. How did those times make you feel?

_____

_____

3. What one-to-one time could you spend with your child(ren) to create special memories for them? (Write down a similar plan for any additional children.)

- I plan to give (state amount of time and frequency)

    _____

    doing (state activity) _____

    with (state child) _____

- I plan to give (state amount of time and frequency)

    _____

    doing (state activity) _____

    with (state child or children) _____

Exercise 4

Giving children responsibility

(Only complete this exercise if you have a child who is old enough to take on responsibility for some household chores.)

Write a list of household chores your child(ren) could do (or help with) appropriate to their age.

Child	Age	Responsibilities
eg: John	3	Tidying up toys before bathtime
eg: Keira	9	Laying the table
		Helping with washing up after meals
		Putting own bicycle into shed

3 Setting Boundaries

Review

Session – Building Strong Foundations

What is a family for?
- a family provides support
- a family provides fun
- a family provides a moral compass
- a family provides a model for relating to others

Establishing a healthy family life
- healthy play
- healthy bonding
- healthy routines
  - daily: mealtimes/bedtimes
  - weekly: creating a family time to have fun together

Session 2 – Meeting our Children's Needs

- our children have 'emotional tanks' that need to be kept full of love
- five ways of showing love through
  - affirming words
  - affectionate touch
  - special time
  - thoughtful presents
  - kind actions

'Those who love their children are careful to discipline them.'

Proverbs 13:24
The Bible

'Parents, do not exasperate your children; instead bring them up in the training and instruction of the Lord.'

Ephesians 6:4, The Bible

Part 1 Combining love and limits

Why do we set boundaries?

- the foundation of effective discipline is unconditional love
- a child growing up wants and needs to know where the boundaries are and who is going to enforce them
- discipline develops three things:
  1) self-discipline (for morally responsible behaviour)
  2) a respect for authority (parental and other)
  3) a sense of security

Where do we set boundaries?

- extremes are dangerous – either in harshness or permissiveness
- create a balance
- aim to be authoritative rather than authoritarian, indulgent or neglectful

Four parenting styles

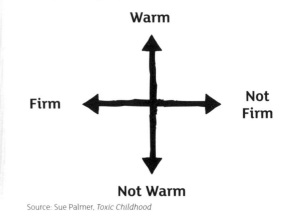

Source: Sue Palmer, *Toxic Childhood*

Examples of the different parenting styles:

1. Richard, aged ten, wants to rent a certificate age fifteen DVD that his friends have been talking about.

   - the neglectful parent would _____

   - the authoritarian parent would _____

   - the indulgent parent would _____

   - the authoritative parent would _____

2. Annie, aged four, has snatched a ball from Sarah, another child of the same age, in the playground

   - the authoritarian parent would _____

   - the indulgent parent would _____

   - the neglectful parent would _____

   - the authoritative parent would _____

How do we set boundaries?

1. Right and wrong choices

- teach the difference between acceptable and unacceptable behaviour
- explain the consequences – pleasant for good behaviour and unpleasant for crossing the boundary
- tell them that the choice is theirs
- teaches them to take responsibility for their own actions

- reward 'right choices' with descriptive praise
- use a 'star chart' or the equivalent for persistent issues
- have negative consequences for 'wrong choices'

2. Choose the right battles

- pause for thought
- stop to think about whether your child is:

H _____

A _____

L _____

T _____

- or, are you?

3. Recognise natural childishness

- recognise the difference between natural childishness and disobedience
- halves the battles we have to fight
- adjust your expectations according to their level of maturity

4. Maintain a sense of humour

- find ways to lighten the atmosphere
- laugh together and with other parents

For 5- and 10-week courses
Exercise

Natural childishness

Think of some examples of natural childishness at different ages. Then discuss what you have put down with one or two others.

Age of child   **Example**
eg: 2   *distracted by older brother and knocks over cup of milk*

· _____   _____

· _____   _____

· _____   _____

What is the best way to react to these examples of childishness? Could humour help?

· _____

· _____

· _____

For 10-week course only
Small group discussion

1. Which style of parenting do you tend to adopt? Is this because of the way you were parented?

_____

_____

Please turn over ⇨

Exercise (continued)

2. What helps you to choose the right battles?

_____

_____

3. What can you do to help reinforce 'right choices'?

_____

_____

4. What consequences could you put in place for 'wrong choices'?

_____

_____

Homework – complete **Exercise 1** on page 44–45

Part 2 – Helping our children make good choices

1. Be fair and clear
   - are they old enough to understand our instructions?
   - are we expecting too much for their age?

2. Use your voice effectively
   - use a serious tone of voice to teach what 'no' means
   - aim not to shout unless warning of danger

3. Action gets results
   - shouting and threatening are ineffective

- important to take action over bad behaviour, *ie: follow through with a consequence*

4. Be one step ahead

- use distraction, *eg: distract your child from the issue causing conflict*
- develop your own family rules to avoid regular arguments

5. Give choices

- being given choices is an important part of a child's learning to take responsibility
- give choices over issues that are unimportant, *eg: 'Which of your toys do you want to take?'* and *'Do you want to play on the beach or go swimming?'*
- giving choices helps to defuse conflict

6. Stay in control

- avoid being dragged into slanging matches
- our emotional reactions can give children a sense of power over us – like allowing them to press a 'big red button' on our chests to see us react, *eg: getting angry, chasing them, getting upset*
- find a way to give realistic warnings
- don't be manipulated by your child(ren)'s shouting, whining or tantrums

7. Follow through with consequences

- don't use idle threats – only give warnings that you can follow through with
- work out effective consequences

8. Work together

- when both parents are involved:
  - agree on a strategy (may require compromise)
  - be consistent
  - support each other

For 5-week course only
Small group discussion

1. Of the four parenting styles – neglectful, authoritarian, indulgent, authoritative
   – which style do you tend to adopt? Is this because of the way you were parented?

_____

_____

2. With your own child(ren), what are the most difficult situations when discipline
   is required?

_____

_____

3. What could help you to reinforce 'right choices'?

_____

_____

4. What consequences could you put in place for 'wrong choices'?

_____

_____

5. What could help you to choose the right battles?

_____

_____

6. How can you stay in control of yourself when faced with bad behaviour?

_____

_____

Homework – complete **Exercises 1** and **2** on pages 44–46

For 10-week course only
Small group discussion

1. With your own child(ren), what are the most difficult situations when discipline is required?

_____

_____

2. Which principles from this session are most helpful in tackling these situations?

_____

_____

3. How can you stay in control of yourself when faced with bad behaviour?

_____

_____

Homework – complete **Exercise 2** on pages 45–46

Homework ✏

Exercise 1

Combining warmth and firmness

1. Think back to your own childhood and the way you were parented as a child. Which of the four styles of parenting did your parent(s)/step-parent(s) use mainly:

   ☐ neglectful (low on both warmth and firmness)?

   ☐ authoritarian (low on warmth, high on firmness)?

   ☐ indulgent (high on warmth, low on firmness)?

   ☐ authoritative (high on both warmth and firmness)?

2. Do you find yourself copying or reacting against the way you were parented?

_____

3. What would you like to do differently with your child(ren)?

_____

_____

4. Think about HALT (hungry, anxious, lonely, tired). Do any of these regularly apply to your child(ren) when they are behaving badly?

   ☐ Hungry   ☐ Anxious   ☐ Lonely   ☐ Tired

5. What could you do to change these situations?

_____

_____

Exercise 1 (continued)

6. Do any of them regularly apply to you?

☐ Hungry   ☐ Anxious   ☐ Lonely   ☐ Tired

7. In what ways could you look after yourself better to be more effective as a
   parent? (*eg: more sleep, a regular break, some exercise, consult a doctor, find
   adult company*)

_____

_____

(see Chapter 2 in *The Parenting Book* for more suggestions on finding support)

Exercise 2

Encouraging right choices

1. What choices have you given your child(ren) today?

_____

_____

2. What encouragement (pleasant consequences) have you given for 'right choices'
   this week?

_____

_____

Please turn over ⇨

Exercise 2 (continued)

3. What unpleasant consequences have you used for 'wrong choices' this week?

_____

_____

4. Can you think of an issue where you could work together more effectively as parents?

_____

Discuss the issue and try to agree on a joint approach.
(You might need to brainstorm possible ideas and choose one to try out. Review how it is working after a few days/weeks.)

Possible approaches: 1. _____

2. _____

3. _____

4. _____

Our agreed approach for now (choose the best idea from above): _____

4

Teaching Healthy Relationships

Review

Session 1 – Building Strong Foundations

What is a family for?
- a family provides support
- a family provides fun
- a family provides a moral compass
- a family provides a model for relating to others

Establishing a healthy family life
- healthy play
- healthy bonding
- healthy routines
  - daily: mealtimes/bedtimes
  - weekly: creating a family time to have fun together

Session 2 – Meeting our Children's Needs

- our children have 'emotional tanks' that need to be kept full of love
- five ways of showing love through
  - affirming words
  - affectionate touch
  - special time
  - thoughtful presents
  - kind actions

Session 3 – Setting Boundaries

- the importance of setting appropriate boundaries for our children

- boundaries for behaviour develop a child's self-discipline, respect for authority and security
- show warmth and firmness (the authoritative style of parenting)
- distinguish between disobedience and natural childishness
- make sure there are pleasant consequences, such as praise, for your child's right choices
- give an unpleasant consequence such as 'time out' for your child's wrong choices
- work together as parents

Discuss:

Think of an example of a boundary you needed to impose this week. What was the result?

Part 1 Modelling and practising relationships

The power of listening

1. Pay full attention

- recognise the important moments to show you are listening
- maintain eye contact

2. Show an interest

- involves effort and generosity
- listen to what appeals to your child(ren)

3. Avoid shutting them down

- value their ideas
- allow them to express negative feelings such as disappointments, embarrassments, sadness, anxiety and anger

4. Reflect back

- repeat back to your child what you think he or she is saying
- reflect back to your child some of his or her words, but not in parrot fashion, as that can be annoying
- concentrate on reflecting back the feelings you think your child is trying to express, *eg: 'it sounds like you feel upset, or frustrated or sad?'*
- reflective listening will help your child(ren) to name their own feelings

Relationships with siblings and other children

1. Don't compare

- value each child for his/her uniqueness
- avoid labelling
- don't make one look good by putting another down

2. Don't try to arbitrate every fight

- give them space to sort out their own disagreements
- remain impartial – don't always blame the older child or jump to conclusions
- intervene if they are hurting each other
- don't allow unkind words or bullying
- think ahead for regular issues that cause disputes: use rotas where possible

3. Have time together as a family

- don't always eat separately
- don't have several TVs in the house
- organise family nights, family outings, family holidays
- do chores together
- allow them to have fun together, playing childish games, being silly, playing outside
- don't always entertain them; allow them to be bored so they make up their own games
- have fun together as a family

4. Give each child space and some privacy

- some children need more time on their own than others

5. Help them to see each other's good points

- give them a sense of responsibility to look out for each other

---

For 5- and 10-week courses
Exercise

Reflective Listening

1. What feelings might lie behind these remarks by children?

1. *'I'm not going back to school ever again. I hate school.'*
2. *'Our team won the match!'*
3. *'Myra and Rupak wouldn't play with me. They said I wasn't big enough to play their game.'*
4. *'Everyone else in my class is better at drawing than me.'*
5. *'Jack has broken my new car.'*
6. *'We lost the football match. I was the goalie and I let in three goals.'*
7. *'I want to go too. I'm easily old enough.'*
8. *'I hate Sam. I don't want to play with him again.'*

In pairs, one of you pretends to be the child (aged between 5 and 10) and the other pretends to be the child's parent. The 'child' says one of the remarks above The 'parent' reflects back what the child might be feeling. Avoid giving advice or reassurance – that may be appropriate later.

eg: Child: 'Everyone else in my class is better at drawing than me.'
Parent: 'It sounds like you find drawing difficult.'

The 'child' then indicates whether or not the 'parent' has understood. The 'parent' reflects back again.

eg: Child: 'Yes, I can never do what the teacher tells us to do.'
Parent: 'That must be annoying for you.'

Continue the conversation for a minute or two. Then swap roles. Use another of the remarks and follow the instructions above.

When you've finished, discuss what it felt like to be listened to as the 'child' and how easy or difficult you found it as the 'parent' to reflect back the child's feelings.

2. Are there any unhelpful habits you've got into where you are favouring one child over another? *eg: listening more attentively to a child who is more articulate than a brother or sister*

_____

For 10-week courses only
Small group discussion

1. What did it feel like to be listened to in the exercise *Reflective Listening*?

_____

_____

2. What could help you to listen effectively to your child(ren), particularly when they are expressing negative emotions such as hurt, anger, disappointment or sadness?

_____

_____

3. What are the main causes of arguments between your children?
(If you only have one child, think about the questions below in relation to your child's friendships with other children.)

_____

_____

Please turn over ⇨

4. What helps them to get on together?

_____

_____

Homework – complete **Exercise 1** on page 57–58

Part 2 Handling anger (ours and theirs)

Unhelpful reactions to anger

- some people react like a rhino
  - when angry, they go on the attack and express their feelings aggressively
- some people react like a hedgehog
  - when angry, they protect themselves and bury their feelings

Learning to control our anger

1. Recognise the root of our anger

- HALT – ask: Am I Hungry, Anxious, Lonely or Tired?
- displaced anger: buried anger caused by someone in the past can come out in the present against someone else
- deal with unresolved hurt from the past through forgiveness

2. Take time out to calm down

- press the pause button
- avoid jumping to conclusions

3. Label the action not the child's character

- avoid phrases like 'You're so careless' or 'You're so unkind'
- children can believe labels

- labelling the action helps them to change, *eg: 'That was a careless thing to do'* or *'That was an unkind remark to make'*

4. Use 'I' statements to express own feelings

- helps us to avoid labelling other people
- easier for them to respond constructively and make changes in their behaviour

Helping our children manage their anger

Toddler tantrums

- normal toddler behaviour between twenty months and four years old
- you are not a bad parent
- remember HALT
- think ahead – distractions, choices, routines
- when faced with full-on tantrum
  - assume impassive face and body language
  - if in public, stay close or hold with firm hug till anger subsides
  - once over don't show too much relief

Older children (5–10 years old)

- read each child's way of showing anger
- aim to teach them 'expression', rather than 'aggression' or 'suppression'
- help them to express anger appropriately (verbally and pleasantly)
- correct rudeness, destructive behaviour, swearing, hitting others, etc – without shutting them down
- allow them to express negative feelings: hurt, sadness, anger, etc
- not allowing expression or discussion can lead to passive aggressive behaviour, *ie: using negative behaviour to get back at parents, such as being uncommunicative, refusing to co-operate, or being deliberately annoying*
- we need to recognise if we are contributing to the problem and our child's anger

- don't punish for being immature in expressing negative feelings

Teaching our children to manage their anger

1. Recognise it's a long process

- typically it takes at least eighteen years!
- help them to realise that talking through an issue that has upset them is more productive than behaving badly

2. Try to find the root cause of the anger

- listen to your child
- HALT – are they Hungry, Anxious, Lonely or Tired?
- may not be easy to work out root cause – they may not know
- if we don't find the root cause, they can become angrier or suppress their emotions, leading to rebellion later
- create environment of openness and honesty to encourage communication

3. Model how to resolve conflict well

- allow your children to see you, as adults, resolving conflict and making up
- when *we* make mistakes as parents, we must say sorry to our children
- when *they* make mistakes, we must forgive
- don't allow hurt and buried anger to fester

For 5-week course only

Small group discussion

1. Do you tend to react more like a rhino or a hedgehog?

_____

_____

2. What helps you to express your anger constructively?

_____

_____

3. How does each child tend to react when angry?

_____

_____

4. What can you do to help them express their anger effectively?

_____

_____

5. What could help you to listen effectively to your child(ren), particularly when they are expressing negative emotions such as hurt, anger, disappointment or sadness?

_____

_____

Please turn over ⇨

6. What helps your children to get on with each other?

_____

_____

Homework – complete **Exercises 1** and **2** on pages 57–60

For 10-week course only
Small group discussion

1. Do you tend to react more like a rhino or a hedgehog?

_____

_____

2. What helps you to express your anger constructively?

_____

_____

3. How does each child tend to react when angry?

_____

_____

4. What can you do to help your child(ren) express his or her anger effectively?

_____

_____

5. How could you give your child(ren) a good model for resolving conflict?

Homework – complete **Exercise 2** on pages 58–60

Homework 🖋

Exercise 1

Acknowledging feelings

- Look at the comments made by children
- Against each one, think of a word that describes what he or she might be feeling
- Then make up a response using that word to show you understand their feelings and to help them to give a name to their feelings
- Avoid giving advice or reassurance – that can come later

Child's comment	Child's feeling (one word)	Parent's response
Example		
'The bus driver shouted at me and everybody laughed.'	*Embarrassment*	*'Sounds as if that was embarrassing'*
1. 'I'd like to punch Michael on the nose!'		
2. 'Just because it rained a little my teacher said we couldn't go on our school trip. She's silly.'		
3. 'Kaylie invited me to her party, but I don't know …'		
4. 'I don't know why teachers have to give us so much homework over the weekend!'		

Please turn over ⇨

Exercise 1 (contnued)

Child's comment	Child's feeling (one word)	Parent's response
5. 'We had football practice today and I kept letting the goals in.'		
6. 'Cheryl is moving away and she's my best friend.'		

Exercise 2

Helping children deal with their anger

☑ any of the ideas that could help you deal with the following situations:

1. *Your two children are in the car. They both want to look at the same book. As they fight, the book drops on the floor. The yelling is very loud, and one of them starts to hit the other. The other hits back and scratches the first one. They are now furious and you can barely concentrate on driving.*

☐ stop the car as soon as possible and take away the book

☐ tell them they can only have the book back if they stop fighting and take it in turns

☐ ask them to say sorry to each other

☐ turn the radio on LOUD and try to ignore them

☐ suggest a game like 'I spy' to distract their attention from the book

☐ another idea _____

Exercise 2 (contnued)

2. *Your 5-year-old is happily playing with his Lego and building an intricate castle. It's time to go out. He refuses to come. You tell him he must come – NOW! He says, 'No,' firmly. You tell him he has no option. He reacts by lying on the floor kicking and then, in a fit of temper, takes a swipe at his castle and destroys it. He is now very cross and also upset that his castle and hard work are ruined.*

☐ pick him up and leave, and allow him to calm down

☐ tell him you will help him build another castle when you return, and then pick him up and leave

☐ explain calmly that he will have to pick up the lego when you return, and then leave

☐ decide that next time you will give him a 5-minute warning before it is time to leave

☐ another idea _____

3. *Your 8-year-old son has come back from school in a bad mood. 'What's up?' you ask. 'Nothing,' he says. 'Go away.' He then proceeds to kick toys on the floor and poke the baby. You can see he is upset but his behaviour is unacceptable. You ask him what happened at school today and he replies rudely, 'I'm not telling you.' He goes upstairs and starts kicking doors and throwing a ball against an upstairs window.*

☐ give him fifteen minutes or so to calm down and then try to find out what's wrong

☐ tell him you understand he's upset but ask him not to break or damage anything. Offer him something soft to throw as an alternative to the ball

☐ tell him he has to stay in his room until he's ready to talk without throwing things around or hurting anyone

☐ ask again at bedtime what was upsetting him and then talk to him about why his behaviour earlier was unacceptable

☐ another idea _____

Please turn over ▷

4. *You are in the supermarket and you are tired! Your 3-year-old is in the shopping trolley – also tired! You start putting food items in the trolley. She sees chocolate biscuits in the aisle and says, 'Want one.' You tell her she can have a biscuit later at home. She sees crisps and shouts, 'I want them.' You tell her she cannot have them. She starts to get cross. She then spies another child in a trolley eating sweets and starts to wail at full volume.*

☐ ignore the screams and smile at other shoppers demonstrating that this situation is entirely normal and you are in full control

☐ tell her that if she stops wailing she can have a box of raisins

☐ try to distract her by asking her advice on which yogurts you should buy and which one she would like for tea

☐ make up a new supermarket game, such as 'Do you think we might see a dog/granny/a man with glasses/a bear in the next aisle?' (being aware that this ploy might only give five minutes of calm)

☐ next week, decide to do your supermarket shop when she is not so tired and agree with her beforehand what she is allowed to eat while you shop, *eg: the end of a baguette or some grapes*

☐ another idea _____

5

Our Long-Term Aim

Review

Session 1 – Building Strong Foundations

What is a family for?
- a family provides support
- a family provides fun
- a family provides a moral compass
- a family provides a model for relating to others

Establishing a healthy family life
- healthy play
- healthy bonding
- healthy routines
  - daily: mealtimes/bedtimes
  - weekly: creating a family time to have fun together

Session 2 – Meeting Our Children's Needs

- our children have 'emotional tanks' that need to be kept full
- five ways of showing love through
  - affirming words
  - special time
  - affectionate touch
  - thoughtful presents
  - kind actions

Session 3 – Setting Boundaries

- boundaries for behaviour develop a child's security, a respect of authority and

self- discipline
- show warmth and firmness
- 'right' choices and 'wrong' choices
- work together as parents

Session 4 – Teaching Healthy Relationships
- our child(ren) will learn more from what we do than what we say
- model effective communication – listen to them, talk about feelings, help them express their feelings
- help them express anger appropriately
- let them see you resolve conflict
- model apologies and forgiveness
- allow them to practise resolving conflict with siblings and other children

Part 1 Encouraging responsibility

Training our children for healthy independence
- we don't own our children
- we are helping our children move from parental control to self-control
- letting them go can be hard for parents
- a gradual process over eighteen years
- allow them to make their own decisions and learn from their own mistakes
- unhealthy control can be caused by wanting to look good, fear of failure, stress or perfectionism

Symptoms of unhealthy control

1. Micro-managing our children's lives
- 'helicopter parenting' – hovering over our children
- children don't learn how to think for themselves

2. Being over-competitive for our children
- puts undue pressure on children

3. Over-scheduling our children's lives

- can be caused by fear that our children will be left out or left behind

4. Over-protecting and rescuing our children

- leads to children not taking responsibility or learning from their mistakes
- allow children to take increasing responsibility for themselves
- pass on information and values to give them a moral framework to live by

Helping children make good choices

1. Sex

- drip-feed information
- answer their questions
- use opportunities for conversations, *eg: magazine articles, TV programmes, films, etc*
- talk about 'right and wrong touch'
- give them a helpful book to read before they reach puberty and offer to discuss it with them

2. The Internet and electronic games

- alert children to the benefits and dangers
- put filters on home computers
- keep computers in family room
- enforce time limits for being online and playing games

Notes

SMART rules for staying safe online

(to discuss with your child)

S SAFE – Keep safe by being careful not to give out personal information when you're chatting or posting online. Personal information includes your email address, phone number and password.

M MEETING – Meeting someone you have only been in touch with online can be dangerous. Only do so with your parents' or carers' permission and, even then, only when they can be present. Remember online friends are still strangers even if you have been talking to them for a long time.

A ACCEPTING – Accepting emails, IM messages, or opening files, pictures or texts from people you don't know or trust can lead to problems – they may contain viruses or nasty messages.

R RELIABLE – Someone online might lie about who he or she is and information on the internet may not be true. Always check information with other websites, books or someone who knows. Chatting online is best done only with your real-world friends and family.

T TELL – Tell your parent, carer or a trusted adult if someone or something makes you feel uncomfortable or worried, or if you or someone you know is being bullied online.

3. Drugs and alcohol

- have conversations throughout their upbringing
- equip them with the facts to inform and protect them

Exercise

Letting go gradually

1. How much time do you allow your children to play by themselves on average each day?

   _____ minutes a day

2. Try to think of three ways you are encouraging increasing independence in your children as they grow up:

   i. _____

   ii. _____

   iii. _____

3. When did you last enable your child(ren) to learn from one of their mistakes?

   _____

4. Do you recognise a tendency in yourself towards unhealthy control in

   ☐ micro-managing your children's lives?

   ☐ being over-competitive for your children?

   ☐ over-scheduling your children's lives?

   ☐ over-protecting and rescuing your children?

   If you put ☑ to any of the above, what could you do to change?

   _____

   _____

Discuss what you have put down with one or two others.

For 10-week course only
Small group discussion

1. Which part of the exercise 'Letting go gradually' was most helpful for you to think about?

_____

_____

2. How can you allow your child(ren) to learn from their mistakes while still protecting them sufficiently?

_____

_____

3. How can you try to pass on your values about sex to your child(ren) as they grow up?

_____

_____

4. What should you do to restrict your child(ren)'s time online and when playing computer games, and how can you help to keep them safe? (See the SMART guidelines in the notes for ideas)

_____

_____

5. How can you try to give your children a healthy attitude towards drugs and alcohol?

_____

_____

Homework – complete **Exercises 1** and **2** on pages 73–74

Part 2 Passing on beliefs and values

How do we pass on our beliefs and values?

- our values are what we consider most important and will be reflected in how we spend our time, money and energy
- what values are we modelling to our children?
- 'notional values' and 'real values'
- our values come from our core beliefs

1. Answering our children's questions

- gives children a framework for understanding what life is about
- why are we here?
- what happens when we die?
- is there a God?

2. Our home environment

- make your home a place that your children want to come back to, where:
    - they are free to be individuals not in a straightjacket of conformity
    - there are boundaries but not legalism
    - there is discipline but not authoritarianism
    - there is more encouragement than criticism
    - there is plenty of fun and laughter
    - there is more gratitude than complaining and blaming
    - there are apologies and forgiveness and the opportunity for fresh starts
- faith is more easily caught than taught
- children initially form their picture of God from the way their parents treat them
- show unconditional love

3. Involving other people

- the wider family
- other role models

4. Passing on our values about money

- pressures on children and parents from advertising and the celebrity culture
- give them choices with pocket money
  - choosing how much to save, spend and give away
- teach generosity, good management and honesty
- help them learn the value of experiencing delayed gratification
- model a healthy attitude towards possessions

5. Praying for our children

- never too soon to start (see the account of John the Baptist in the womb in Luke 1:44, The Bible)
- never too late to start (see the Parable of the Lost Son in Luke 15:11-24, The Bible)
- turn fears and longings into prayers
- when to pray:
  - with them before they go to sleep
  - teaching them to pray ('thank you', 'sorry', 'please')
  - on our own
  - with others
  - in traffic jams or when doing the washing up or ironing
  - when prompted (often at moments of potential danger or temptation for our child)
  - everyday
- what to pray for:
  - friendships
  - schools
  - their health
  - their safety
  - their marriage partner (most children will marry one day and their marriage partner may well already be alive somewhere)
  - their response to God's love
  - their characters – use the fruit of the Spirit as a list to pray through: 'love, joy, peace,

patience, kindness, goodness, faithfulness, gentleness and self-control'
(see Galatians 5:22-23, The Bible)
- pray with them, particularly at bedtime
- pray for yourselves as parents

6. Developing family traditions, routines and rituals

- traditions create a family identity
- help our children feel they belong
- positive traditions reinforce our values
- our children will be more secure and better able to resist peer pressure when necessary
- daily routines (see Session 1)
- weekly traditions
    - family night (see Session 1)
    - weekends
    - church going
- annual traditions
    - family holidays
    - birthdays
    - Christmas and other festivals
    - marking the seasons

Family traditions and rituals

1. What are your own daily, weekly or annual traditions and rituals?

Daily:

1. _____

2. _____

3. _____

Weekly:

1. _____

2. _____

3. _____

Annual:

1. _____

2. _____

3. _____

2. Do you have any 'negative' traditions that need to be dropped? *(eg: a tradition that is detrimental to a child or to your family life, such as having every meal in front of the TV)*

_____

3. From this session's talk and discussion with other parents, what new rituals could you develop?

Daily: _____

Weekly: _____

Annual: _____

4. What values regarding money do you want to pass on to your children?

_____

Homework – complete **Exercises 1–3** on pages 73–74

For 10-week course
Small group discussion

Family traditions and rituals

1. What are your own daily, weekly or annual traditions and rituals?

Daily:

i. _____

ii. _____

iii. _____

Weekly:

i. _____

ii. _____

iii. _____

Please turn over ⇨

Annual:

i. _____

ii. _____

iii. _____

2. Do you have any 'negative' traditions that need to be dropped? *(eg: a tradition that is detrimental to a child or to your family life, such as having every meal in front of the TV)*

_____

3. From this session's talk and discussion with other parents, what new rituals could you develop?

Daily: _____

Weekly: _____

Annual: _____

4. What values regarding money do you want to pass on to your children?

_____

Homework – complete **Exercise 3** on page 74

Homework ✎

Exercise 1

Building character

Try to write down the most important values/character traits you would like to see in your children in order of importance.
(eg: kindness, loyalty, self-control, optimism, honesty, happiness, sense of humour, courtesy, gratitude, respect, generosity, humility and gentleness)

1. _____

2. _____

3 _____

4. _____

5. _____

Exercise 2

Passing on beliefs and values

1. What are the most important beliefs and values you want to pass on to your children?

_____

_____

2. How can you best model these?

_____

_____

Please turn over ▷

Exercise 2 (continued)

3. What are the other ways you can help to pass them on?

_____

_____

Exercise 3

Parenting goals

Write down the three most important things you've learnt/been reminded of on The Parenting Children Course.

1. _____

2. _____

3 _____

Write down three changes you have made/would like to make as a result.

1. _____

2. _____

3 _____

The Parenting Children Course sofa families

We are very grateful to the parents and children who agreed to appear on the DVDs and talk about their own experiences of parenting or being parented. The names in **bold** are the family members who feature.

Annie and **Silas**
Jessie (19) Zac (18) Mo (16) Minnie (15) Tallulah (13)

Barbara and Sam
Samuel (6)

Con and Madeleine
Henry (15) **Amelia (12)** Tom (11) **Charlie (7)** Johnnie (18 mths)

Dianne and Alan
Neil (12) Jacob (10) Oliver (4)
Dianne and Alan's three boys are all adopted.

Eli and Jon
Noelle (15) Jocosa (2)
Eli raised Noelle as a single parent for many years. She is now married to Jon, and Jocosa is their child.

John and Krista
Owen (10) Matt (8)
John and Krista have four other children from previous marriages between the ages of 17 and 20.

Joy
Abigail (11) Joshua (9) **Hannah (8)**
Joy is a single parent.

Karen and Paul
Liam (23) Christian (21) Hannah (18)

Mandie and **Mark**
Matthew (8) Emma (6)

Niyi and **Oyinkan**
Tosin (13) Obafemi (9) Adeolu (6)

Pandora
Four adult children
Pandora is a single parent.

Paul and **Philomena**
Patrick (16) **Emily (15) Johnnie (11) Max (10)**

Phil and **Ici**
Lauren (10) Lukas (10) Josiah (7)
Lukas is Ici's nephew, and he now lives with them as a part of their immediate family.

Rachel and **Sam**
Caleb (6) Levi (4) Talitha (6 months)

Sam and **Archie**
Charlie (9) Genie (7) **Joel (6)** Theo (3)

Shona
Ashlyn (6) RJ (3)
Shona is a single parent.

Sijeong and **Woodug**
Eunchan (4) Eunchae (2)

Please turn over ⇨

Taryn and **Mark**
Caleb (6) Ella (4) Asher (2)

Tony
Ciara (13) Orla (11) Ruairi (7)
Tony is a single parent and a widower.

Will and Ali
Bart (8) Fergus (6)

Appendix 2

Parenting experts

We are very grateful to the following parenting 'experts' who have generously contributed to the DVDs. Please find below contact details for them or their organisation and some of their publications.

Harry Benson – founder of Bristol Community Family Trust; involved with family policy, research and relationship courses; author of *Let's Stick Together: The Relationship Book For New Parents*. **bcft.co.uk**

Lucinda Fell – Director of Policy and Communications at Childnet International, a non-profit organisation helping to make the Internet a great and safe place for children and teenagers. To access Childnet's wide range of resources to support parents and carers see the websites **childnet.com** and **kidsmart.org**

Glynis Good – Couple and families relationship counsellor in Dublin, Ireland, with particular concern for supporting young people through the difficult impact of parental separation; author of *When Parents SPLIT: Support, information and encouragement for teenagers*. **whenparentssplit.com**

Julie Johnson – PSHE consultant and trainer; provider of parenting workshops in and around the London area, UK; child and adolescent family counsellor; Human Givens therapist; specialist in issues surrounding growing up and adolescence, bullying, loss and change, including bereavement and parental separation; author of *Being Angry*, *Bullies and Gangs* (both part of the *Thoughts and Feelings* series for children aged 5–10, published by Franklin Watts) and *How Do I Feel About My Stepfamily*. **julie.johnson@virgin.net**

Timothy Johns – Headmaster, The Hawthorns School, Bletchingly, Surrey RH1 4QJ, a co-educational day school for children aged 2–13

Sue Palmer – Former headteacher; educationalist and educational consultant specialising in literacy training; author of *Toxic Childhood*, *Detoxing Childhood* and *21st Century Boys* **suepalmer.co.uk**

Rob Parsons – Chairman and founder of Care for the Family; author of *The Sixty Minute Father* and *Teenagers: what every parent has to know*, among other parenting titles; international speaker on family life and business. See **careforthefamily.org.uk** for further resources supporting many areas of family life

Please turn over ⇨

Dr Aric Sigman – Psychologist; biologist; broadcaster; business speaker; author of *Remotely Controlled: How television is damaging our lives*, *The Spoilt Generation: Why restoring authority will make our children and society happier* and *Alcohol Nation: How to protect our children from today's drinking culture* **aricsigman.com**

Dr Pat Spungin – Child psychologist and family life specialist; author of *Silent Nights, The Haynes Teenager Manual: The practical guide for all parents*, *The Parentalk Guide to Brothers and Sisters* (co-authored with Victoria Richardson) and *Understand Your Family* (Consultant Editor) **drpatspungin.co.uk**

Appendix 3

Recommended reading

The book of the course:

The Parenting Book
by Nicky & Sila Lee (Alpha International, 2009)

Other books, alphabetical by author:

The Children's Bible in 365 Stories
by Pat Alexander (Lion, 2001)

How to Really Love Your Child
by Ross Campbell, M.D. (Cook
Communications Ministries, 1992)

*Anger: Handling a Powerful Emotion in a
Healthy Way*
by Gary Chapman (Northfield Publishing,
2007)

The Five Love Languages of Children
by Gary Chapman and Ross Campbell, M.D.
(Northfield Publishing, 1997)

Who Made Me?
by Malcolm & Meryl Doney (Candle Books,
2006)

What is God's Design for My Body?
by Susan Horner (Moody Publishers, 2004)

The Marriage Book
by Nicky & Sila Lee (Alpha International,
2009)

Toxic Childhood
by Sue Palmer (Orion Books, 2006)

The Sixty Minute Family
by Rob Parsons (Lion, 2010)

The Sixty Minute Father
by Rob Parsons (Hodder & Stoughton, 1995)

The Sixty Minute Mother
by Rob Parsons (Hodder & Stoughton, 2009)

Baby Boy Bible/Baby Girl Bible
by Sarah Toulmin (Good Books, 2007)

Baby Prayers
by Sarah Toulmin (Good Books, 2008)

relationshipcentral.org

If you are interested in finding out more about
The Parenting Children Course or
The Parenting Teenagers Course, where
they are running or how to start up a course,
please contact:

Relationship Central
HTB Brompton Road
London SW7 1JA
Tel: **0845 644 7533**
Fax: **020 7589 3390**
Email: **info@relationshipcentral.org**
Website: **relationshipcentral.org**

If you are interested in finding out more about
the Christian faith and
would like to be put in touch with your nearest
Alpha course, please contact:

The Alpha Office
HTB Brompton Road
London SW7 1JA
Tel: **0845 644 7544**
Fax: **020 7589 3390**
Email: **ukalpha@alpha.org**
Website: **alpha.org**